What To Know Before

Marketing Your

Clinician, Instruction, or Coaching

Horse

Business

In The New Economy

PATRICIA RESZETYLO

What To Know Before Marketing Your Clinician, Instructing, or Coaching Horse Business In The New Economy

For information contact the author at:

http://PatriciaReszetylo.com

ISBN: 1523345462

ISBN-13: 978-1523345465

3nd Edition: November, 2017

TABLE OF CONTENTS

INTRODUCTION

Dear Equine Clinician, Instructor, or Coach,

What *should* you know before you start marketing your business? Are there things that, if you knew them, would make marketing easy, bring you GREAT clients, and even better, make you MONEY?

Are there things that would totally transform your business?

See, I know a little-known, well-hidden horse industry secret. I know that MOST clinicians are just a few steps away from the street – from being out of business. I know that if you lose the wrong clients, if you don't keep 2 steps ahead of the competition, you're toast.

If you're tired of the never-ending hamster wheel, it's time to transform your business. It won't happen overnight, although you may start to see results very quickly.

YES, I'm suggesting you LITERALLY transform your horse business so completely and transparently that your competition doesn't know what happened. All they know is that you now have all the best clients, horses, and profits - and they are left with the DUDs.

You'll notice as you implement the strategies, that you have so fenced in your own herd of clients, starting with your current ones, and then extending that to your well-indoctrinated prospects that it's *as if* competing businesses don't even exist.

And when we're done, your competition may as well NOT exist, for all the effect they'll have on your business.

Because you *do* want to keep them in business. After all, you need somewhere to refer the clients you no longer want, or the ones that you simply can't take on.

Ok? Let's take this from the top.

You love horses. You always have. And to continue to enjoy them, you market your business.

Maybe you want to offer well-heeled clients, higher-end horses, better accommodations, better training, and attract MORE of the better riders.

Or perhaps your objectives include bringing in better (and more) sponsors.

One of the quickest ways to reach your IDEAL Client (or sponsor – or both) is to do savvy marketing - things your competition does NOT do.

If you do the things they do, how do your potential clients KNOW that they want to come to your business? Copying others' marketing is just marketing incest.

It does NOT differentiate you from your competition, leaving you with the Small Fish/Big Pond Syndrome.

It's also the quickest way to the lowest common denominator, which in marketing is price. Marketing with price as your competitive advantage is the quickest way to run yourself out of business.

Good-bye IDEAL clients, hello DUDS.

Even the big stores, such as Wal-Mart™ who DO compete on price, only do so as a **perception**. They want you to THINK they are the low price leader. Here's a secret: even **they** are abandoning that approach.

They can see where the "low-price leader" path leads.

So can you. So you know you have to do something different.

You may already be working in that direction. That alone makes you an ideal candidate to learn this strategy.

This is by no means a NEW strategy. It is one that has been successfully used for hundreds, if not thousands, of years.

We're going to give your direct competitors "the boot" in the eyes of your clients and your potential clients.. giving YOUR business the *Leg Up* you desire.

Imagine building a competition-proof "fence" around your herd of IDEAL riders and vendors (we'll call these **clients** for simplicity's sake). Now you can do just that. And even better, you can influence potential IDEAL clients that are still outside that fence, and draw them in.

HOW TO USE THIS BOOK

This book is meant to be used as a guidebook to direct you into a high impact-on-your-market strategy. For this strategy to work for you, we compile information which we then leverage, or in some cases, use as markers to show progress.

<u>So find a quiet, comfortable, well-lit place to read – and write</u>. Have a

- <u>Cup of coffee</u> or tea at hand.
- <u>A highlighter</u> – yes, mark this book up. It's YOURS! You learn better when you have stuff highlighted.
- <u>A writing pen</u>, so you can do the Transformation exercises <u>in</u> the book. And do them IN the book – it's all set up for you, and there are real reasons to do the assignments in order – they build on each other.
- You may want to have your bookkeeping and a calculator close at hand. I'll ask you to do some number stuff in some of the Transformation exercises. Don't worry, it's pretty simple stuff.

You may find that it takes several sessions to get through this book, especially as you do the assignments, but you'll come out with a much better view of your business, your target market, what you want to achieve with both your business and your life – and the real capacity of your business!

Don't Wait! Right now, before your competition learns about this, and while I can still offer these sessions, go *directly* to page 88 and apply for your $197 value consultation to start transforming _your_ business from Great to Amazing!

About The Author

I'm Patricia Reszetylo, a life-long equestrian and business student. My best teachers have been a plethora of other business students, including Dr Richard Bandler, Dan S. Kennedy, and Jay Abraham, to name a few of the greats.

I've also ran a number of businesses - of which some were more successful than others, but all of which were learning laboratories, networking and launching boards for future enterprises.

I've been blessed with great horses, great friends, and great marketing minds to call upon.

I'm known in the horse industry for doing teleseminars, webinars, and Google Hangouts long before they were popular.

And now I'm handing YOU a pile of business strategies so brilliant you'd think they were concieved just yesterday.. but most of them weren't. In fact, they've been around for a VERY long time...

Happy Trails!
Patricia Reszetylo,
January, 2016

1

ELIMINATES YOUR COMPETITION

Competition is fierce these days. Even though the economy is coming back into its own, here in early 2015, due to the recent recession, consumers are still skeptical of the claims you make in the marketplace. They want to be sure when they spend money that it brings them real value.

No, they don't trust your claims. With more and more people who believe the government needs to hand out more and more aid; people who believe that "the middle class is shrinking," and that THAT is a BAD thing; even more incidents of those who are supposed to protect us violently accosting innocent bystanders, nobody trusts anybody these days.

Reputation – what others say about you – is much more important, and taken much more seriously than anything you can say about yourself.

In fact, when YOU say something about yourself (about your event), people automatically assume you are hiding something. That's why they ask around about your event, and find out what your reputation is. Social media is both the

Wouldn't it be great if you could:

- ☐ Essentially "**get rid of**" your competition, and charge anything you like?
- ☐ Have your pick of the **best clients and horses** in your market?
- ☐ ***Not*** worry that another, *inferior* clinician or instructor or coach might steal your best clients?
- ☐ Send your **DUD clients** to *other* clinicians?

Well, now you can.

In the little book which you now hold in your hands, I'll show you how to achieve ALL FOUR goals faster and easier than you might imagine.

TRANSFORMATION 1A: Take a pen and check each box in the list above that IS something you'd like to achieve in the next 6-12 months.

TRANSFORMATION 2B: On the lines below, write **what achieving them means to you**:

1. _____

    _____

2. _____

    _____

3. _____

    _____

4. _____

    _____

This is a very important Transformation Item. Don't just skip ahead to the next chapter.

2

Establishes You as an Authority

If you did the first 2 Transformations, congratulate yourself! You've just done more for yourself than most businesses EVER do to make life easy for themselves. **Award yourself a nice, big carrot!**

You didn't? Stop right now, go back to the Transformation, and do your homework! **No carrots for you until you do!**

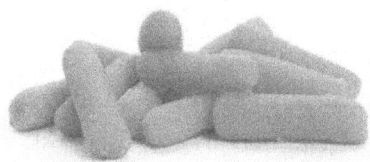

We are swamped with advertising messages. Billboards, advertisements, and marketing statements are everywhere these days. There is NO escaping them. Now that we are connected with our devices, there are even more – and the net result is that we don't pay as much attention to not just the advertising messages, but to anything!

As a business person looking to make a statement in your market, you have to find ways to stand out from the clutter in order to get your message to your market *before* your competition gets their hooks into *your* Ideal Client.

What are the best things to do to achieve that? I find it's a process with 3 basic elements, a complete strategy to implement, rather than just using a tactic here or there:

- Know your **market**
- Craft your **message** to *that* market

- Deliver it via the best **medium** for *that* market.

The best strategies create an ongoing marketing funnel, if you will, that consistently attracts, qualifies, develops, and moves the client forward into your sales process.

Establishing yourself as the foremost authority in your market is an absolutely essential piece of the strategy. In fact, using the above strategy *automatically* sets you up as an authority in your market.

TRANSFORMATION 2: Answer the following questions:

1. What specific market do I want to dominate? Consider the following aspects: geographic, discipline, skill level, age, financials, etc.

   ----

2. What message is most important to communicate to them?

This is a very important Transformation Item. Don't just skip ahead to the next chapter.

NOTES:

3

A SIMPLE SYSTEM FOR THIS YEAR

If you did the first 3 Transformations, congratulate yourself! You've just done more for yourself than most businesses EVER do to make life easy for themselves. **Award yourself a nice, big carrot!**

You didn't? Stop right now, go back to the Transformation, and do your homework! **No carrots for you until you do!**

As an equestrian clinician, instructor, or coach, you can easily spend the next 20-40 (or more) years in training, teaching, competing, and giving clinics in order to set yourself up as an expert or as an authority... and while you might be the best equestrian on the planet, you can still die in obscurity.

Plenty of fabulous equestrians do. And the really sad part of it is that if they were marketed well, more than just a few others would know of them, be able to work with them, learn from them – and pass on what wonderful insights they have.

Instead of dying with so little influence, reach, and connections in the world.

OR you could write (the RIGHT book), market it (the RIGHT way), and establish yourself as an authority *THIS* year.

Why? Because when you're an author, especially of a book, people **automatically** respect you. You are given **opportunities** not extended to regular, mere mortals. People assume you are not only an expert, but THE BEST at what you do.

Only experts write books, right? And it takes years of blood, sweat and tears to write a book.. and pure, unadulterated genius to market it, right?

I'm going to let you in on some of the BEST kept secrets in marketing.

1. **No**, you don't have to be a world-renown expert to write a book.
2. **No**, It doesn't take forever to write a GOOD one, and if it's done right, it doesn't take a river of blood, sweat and tears.
3. **No**, YOU don't have to be the genius marketing it.

Marketing isn't rocket science. It only takes an understanding of who you are trying to reach, what issues they have – and which of those you are able to solve well. It does take a minimal, technical understanding of what is available to use, what that technology can and cannot do, and how people respond to marketing messages (basic psychology).

Thus, when your book is written – *and* marketed – correctly, it turns into one of the BEST lead-generation tools available to modern clinicians.

Yes, there are a few tricks to it, just as there are tricks to teaching an equestrian how to bond with her horse, or as there are to getting your horse to do something YOU want.

And I'll help you connect better with your market than you ever DREAMED possible – I have more than a few tricks up my sleeve, along with a few connections you don't!

TRANSFORMATION 3: 5 Reasons I Want To Be An Authority Figure

Grab your pen, and start writing! Yes, make a list **right here**:

1. _____

2. _____

3. _____

4. _____

5. _____

This is a very important Transformation Item. Don't just skip ahead to the next chapter.

NOTES:

_____

_____

_____

_____

_____

_____

_____

_____

_____

_____

_____

_____

_____

_____

4

No changes in your life?

If you did the first 4 Transformations, congratulate yourself! You've just done more for yourself than most businesses EVER do to make life easy for themselves. __Award yourself a nice, big carrot!__

You didn't? Stop right now, go back to the Transformations, and do your homework! __No carrots for you until you do!__

Our business goals often come from our personal goals.. which then all-too-often take a back seat to the business goal. Now we have clients that need lessons, horses trained and cared for, competed, promoted.. and we forget why we went into business in the first place.

Why did YOU go into business as a clinician, coach or instructor in the horse industry? Was it so you could work 12-18 hour days? Was it so you could be tied to the barn and your clients, with no life of your own?

As equestrians, we usually go into business in the industry because we love horses. We enjoy riding. We enjoy training. We enjoy instructing other equestrians. It's a kick to see people learning and implementing new ideas. We just made a whole ripple of lives better.

We start CHARGING for those services for 2 reasons:

- The client has more respect for the work we do when **they** pay,
- We, like everybody else, have bills to pay.

How much we charge is based on how much <u>we</u> feel we deserve for the activity. If we're insecure, or we don't know how to sell our services, we often charge "only what others are charging." We compete on price. We sell ourselves out.

We're told that "working hard to get what we want" is called "having a work ethic," and that it's a good thing.

It can be. When we work hard, practice what we do best, we get very good at what we do. And THAT is a good thing!

But it can be a BAD thing to put off any kind of easily attainable rewards for that elusive, traditionally acquired carrot of "When you finally are 'established.'"

Why do we have to accept that the standard, traditionally accepted path to authority status is the ONLY path.. <u>especially</u> when there are other paths available?

Let me explain.

Yes, you do need to do GOOD work (The rest is just marketing).

There are people in this world who REALLY stand out. They aren't any better than you are. They didn't have any advantages that you didn't. Why did they get ahead so easily.. and why are you still struggling?

It's likely they took ADVANTAGE of an opportunity that you did not. That is a very easy thing to fix.

Let's get back to our original goals.

We know that setting goals is one of the first things we need to do to achieve them. What are your goals in life? What do you want to achieve for yourself, your business, your family, your clients?

What dreams did you have as a child? How many of those have you achieved? What is in your "bucket list?"

TRANSFORMATION 4: GOAL SETTING

Grab your pen, and start writing! Yes, make a list **right here**:

1. _____

2. _____

3. _____

4. _____

5. _____

6. _____

7. _____

8. _____

9. _____

10. _____

This is a very important Transformation Item. Don't just skip ahead to the next chapter.

NOTES:

5

BREAKS THRU ADVERTISING

If you did the first 5 Transformations, congratulate yourself! You've just done lots more for your business than most businesses EVER do to make life easy for themselves. **Award yourself a nice, big carrot!**

You didn't? Stop right now, go back to the Transformation, and do your homework! **No carrots for you until you do!**

A book is special, as we mentioned, because people now treat *you* differently. You are a *published author*, after all! *They* could never write a book (as if only special people can write books)!

And the media likes to talk about new books too. It's much, *much* easier to get interviews on T.V., radio or with a newspaper when they have a book to talk about than if you were going to get one to talk about you, your business, your stable, your students.

So, first we write an amazing book that your IDEAL customer finds extremely useful. Then we share it with your local media. They don't know about it until we tell them in a unique and creative fashion.

Even before the media asks you for an interview, we set it up so they ask you for background info. How is it that you are this amazing expert that could write this book? That's when you talk about you, your history, your stable, your stallion... whatever it is that you are really trying to market.

So a book is an easy way to get into those interviews in the first place – and then there are wonderful ways to leverage any media exposure so that you can extend the effect.

<u>When dealing with your target market, you'll find that your book, and the resulting media, turns you into a hero, an icon, somebody that people are amazed will talk to them.</u> You'll have people come up to you and ask things like, "Are you that author?" When you affirm you are, they will squeal and laugh and ask for your autograph. YOU haven't changed – their perception of you has changed, and that's what we want.

You think you're just sweaty from cleaning stalls. They say, "She's so down to earth..."

If you've never had a media interview before, don't worry. There are easy ways to make it easy for both YOU and the interviewer. And 90% (or more) aren't even in person. They are done over the phone.

<u>Now, take 5 minutes to write out 5 questions you DO want to answer in a media interview.</u> You can also write down 5 sub topics that we can develop questions around.

TRANSFORMATION 5: Questions I *WANT* to Media To Ask Me:

Yes, take 5-10 minutes to make a list here:

1. _____

2. _____

3. _____

4. _____

5. _____

6

ESTABLISHES TRUST

If you did the first 6 Transformations, congratulate yourself! You've just done lots more for yourself than most businesses EVER do to make life easy for themselves. **<u>Award yourself a nice, big carrot!</u>**

You didn't? Stop right now, go back to the Transformation, and do your homework! **<u>No carrots for you until you do!</u>**

We've just been through the deepest recession since the 70's. Many of your clients may not have even been born then, or if they were around, they don't remember it, as they were just too young to be aware.

<u>I promise you this: They won't forget this one anytime soon.</u>

Millions of people out of work, coupled with millions of overpriced, over-leveraged homes repossessed, made for a scary 5 or 6 years. Many stables, breeding operations and even rescues went under, sending their horses to other rescues... or to slaughter.

I can't count how many "horses in need" posts I saw during that time.

People stopped going to shows, stopped training, and stopped taking riding lessons. Everything came to a screeching halt for many. The middle class had money... but was NOT spending it.

It was a confidence issue, not an availability issue. Things are picking up as I wrote the original version of this book in mid-2014, but for those who've been through this, *they'll never forget it.*

Every purchase has to count. Everything must HAVE measurable value, as compared to pre-recessionary days, where people bought stuff just because it was there.

And even more than that, they have to trust YOU.

Publishing a book has an interesting side effect: it increases your personal perceived value. Now that you have a published book to your name, your interaction with them has more value:

- **You're an established authority**, even more than you were before. What you say and do *means* more, is more important and more valuable.
- **You have "star power."** For example, any pretty girl can sex up a car. But put a celebrity in that same car, and it multiplies the sexiness of it. That is why the star's name is so valuable. The same holds true in your business.
- **You'll attract more of your "best qualified" IDEAL clients** to your business, which means you can let go of your "less qualified" clients. Now you're getting paid better, and doing more of what you love, less of what you don't. Your time is more valuable now!
- **You've established solid reasons for them to trust you** – "After all, she wrote a book on it, she knows what she's talking about."

TRANSFORMATION 6: 4 Ways My New Improved Authority Benefits My Clients:

Yes, take 5-10 minutes to make a list here:

1. _____

2. _____

3. _____

4. _____

NOTES:

_____

_____

_____

_____

_____

_____

_____

_____

_____

_____

_____

_____

7

How To Fire 80% of Your Herd

If you did the first 7 Transformations, congratulate yourself! You've just done lots more for yourself than most businesses EVER do to make life easy for themselves. **Award yourself a nice, big carrot!**

You didn't? Stop right now, go back to the Transformation, and do your homework! **No carrots for you until you do!**

Writing a book and marketing it the way we do is called direct response marketing. Any marketing that does not rely on "brand awareness" or "getting the message in front of prospects many times" might be direct response marketing (DRM). The magic comes from

- understanding the market you are targeting,
- learning what makes them tick,
- knowing what your solution does for them, and then
- using that knowledge along with skilled writing to capture their attention, and get them to act NOW.

Mesmerizing them with pink, clapping bunnies[i] to sell your batteries isn't DRM. Capturing their attention with a great headline, getting your message

---

[1] Which brand of batteries does the bunny sell? **See endnote i**

to resonate with them, and then giving them a great reason to act NOW *is* DRM.

As a small business, you have different values and objectives than a huge national corporation does. They have egos to stroke, and investors to keep happy. You need to focus on keeping your clients happy – and in getting new ones with the most efficiency possible.

When I work with a client to write a book to assist them in marketing their equestrian coaching business, I always start out with a pile of questions:

- What problem(s) do you solve?
- What does your best customer look like?
- Who are your competitors?
- Where do you want to be in 3 years' time?

How do you know who is your best customer? Who spends the most money with you, and at the same time, is the least hassle? With whom do you have the best profit margin? Who do you want more of?

We can look at this from the opposite end too: Who is your DUD customer? Who costs you the most in time and/or money (as time IS money)? Who pays you the least, nitpicks over stuff, gripes over paying (or maybe pays late); insists on cafeteria-style rather than package-based buying? Who gives you the most headaches, and is the biggest pain in the ass?

The Pareto Principle says that 80% of your profits come from 20% of your herd. That means that you can cull much of the 80%, and then you can replace them with more clients like the 20%. Knowing WHO they are is the first step. So I ask, "Which ones would YOU cull?"

TRANSFORMATION 7: WHO'S MY BEST CUSTOMER?

7.A.:Names of some of my best customers over the years (don't worry, this is your book, nobody else will see it):

Yes, make a list here:

1. _____   3. _____

2. _____   4. _____

7.B.: So let's look again at those BEST customers again.

What characteristics do they all have in common? Yes, make a list here:

1. _____

2. _____

3. _____

4. _____

5. _____

Transformation 7.C: What Problem(s) Do I Solve For My Customer?

Take 5-10 minutes to write down problem(s) you solve for your **best** customers:

Yes, make a list here:

1. _____

2. _____

3. _____

This is a very important Transformation Item. Take 10 minutes and do it – don't just skip ahead to the next chapter.

NOTES:_____

_____

_____

_____

8

MULTIPLIES YOUR PROFITS

If you did the first 10 Transformations, congratulate yourself! You've just done lots more for yourself than most businesses EVER do to make life easy for themselves. **Award yourself a nice, big carrot!**

You didn't? Stop right now, go back to the Transformation, and do your homework! **No carrots for you until you do!**

Let's go back to why you need a book, how it should be set up to operate as a direct marketing tool, how to leverage the website so they all work as a powerful marketing strategy.. not just as separate tactics.

First, we use the book to set up a conversation with your BEST potential customer. But we don't set up just **any** conversation – we set up the conversation **WE want them to have**.

We'll use the book to educate them – and even beyond that, to **indoctrinate them** – to your way of thinking, operating, and working. Now you have people a group of people who:

- **Understand and like your process** of riding, training, and/or caring for their horse;

- Can decide if they LIKE it and want to work with you, **or** dislike it, and therefore **won't hassle you** with months of slow death and the cost of your moral before they finally pack up and leave;
- Are literally *inoculated* **mentally** against going to other competing clinicians, trainers or instructors;
- And **are willing to jump through hoops** to get in to work with you.

Your website is one of the hoops they have to jump through in order to work with you. They HAVE to approach you in a specific manner, or they are not qualified to work with you.

Why should we make them jump through hoops to get to you? Why don't we make it easy to get in?

BECAUSE: We want to **disqualify as many as possible**, so you can focus on working with the few who **do** fit your IDEAL Client Profile.

TRANSFORMATION 8.A: Looking at your revenue-producing activities, make a list of the ones that *you enjoy the most*, starting with your favorite, and ending with the least enjoyable.

1. _____

2. _____

3. _____

4. _____

TRANSFORMATION 8.B: Now, disregarding what you just wrote down, order your revenue-producing activities starting with the MOST profitable, and ending with the least.

1. _____

2. _____

3. _____

4. _____

TRANSFORMATION 8.C: Go back to the lists you just made, and make a tick mark beside each item that is on BOTH lists. This is a very important Transformation Item.

Here is another way to look at the last 3 Transformations:

The overlap between your (1) Competency/Enjoyment Area Activities and (2) the MOST profitable activities are (3) where you need to spend most of your time and energy. You'll enjoy the work more, you'll make more money, and your clients will be happier, more likely to stay longer, pay more, and refer more clients like themselves into the business.

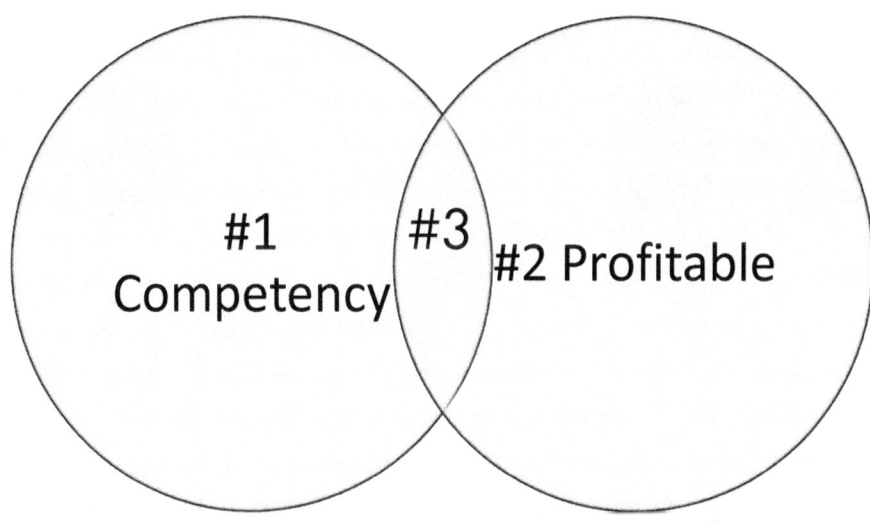

Doing this transformation sets you up for this cycle:

1. You enjoy your work MORE, which allows you to give your herd BETTER service... which leads to more enjoyment for both you AND them.
2. Better service and happier clients leads to more profits, and more referrals, which leads back to happier clients and more enjoyment, in turn leading to a continuous upward cycle.

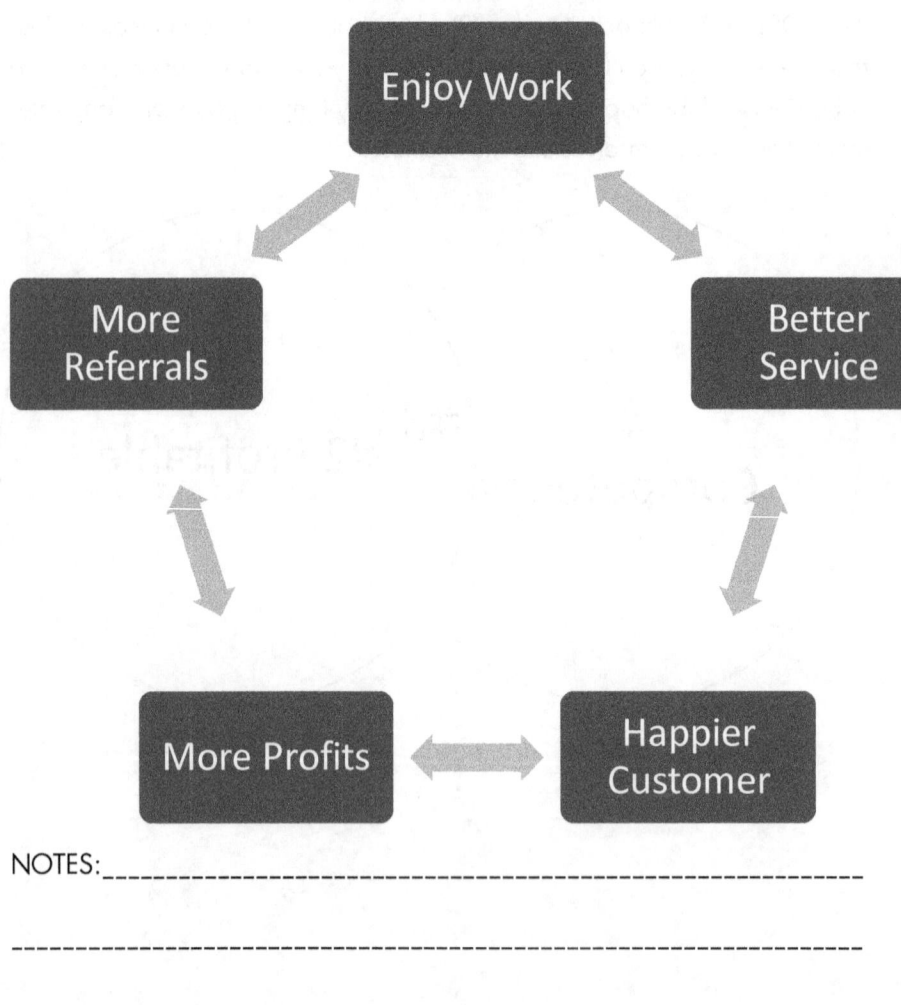

NOTES:_____

_____

9

HOPE MARKETING

If you did the first 12 Transformations, congratulate yourself! You've just done lots more for yourself than most businesses EVER do to make life easy for themselves. **Award yourself a nice, big carrot!**

You didn't? Stop right now, go back to the Transformation, and do your homework! **No carrots for you until you do!**

What is "Hope Marketing"?

Hope Marketing is:

- Thinking that all you have to do is "**hang out your shingle**" and that people will just come and buy your stuff.
- Pretending you're a BIG BRAND, and that big-company **BRANDING-type marketing will make sales**.
- HOPING your marketing is working, even though you aren't tracking it, and **you don't know how people find you**. If they find you at all.
- And worst of all, "Hope Marketing" has been popularized by T.V. and movies. You see so many movies where people put extraordinary effort into things, but the bad guy still repossesses the shop because the owner merely HOPED that her extra special muffins or cookies would do the trick on their own.

The polar opposite of "Hope Marketing" is Direct Response Marketing. This is marketing that:

- <u>KNOWS what the target market is looking for – AND – what words will spur them to Transformation NOW</u>.
- Doesn't concern itself with branding. BRANDING is a happy side effect of good marketing.
- <u>Tracks where people come from</u>, what marketing brought them in, as well as many other stats. It's marketing held accountable for production. If it doesn't *work*, it's *fired*.

Unless you have the need to randomly spend money on helping your ad agency win creative awards, or the need to stroke the egos of stockholders, you need to use Direct Response Marketing (DRM).

Still with me?

Great! Let's carry on!

While there are many strategies and tactics in DRM, it's often best to start with looking at what you are currently doing, and finding ways to add tracking capabilities to it.

<u>Here are some ways to do that:</u>

- Add a "*dept #*" or "*dept. name*" to marketing that uses a mailing address, or which asks the person to make a phone call.
- *Keeping count on a list of your advertising places*, which you tick when a new client calls you, is useful.
- It may also work to *change the offer* you have them ask for, so that the different offers are indicative of where the advert was located.
- *Upgrade your website*. Switching from a "brochure-type" layout to one that forces an optin to your email list, sometimes using an "ethical bribe," is widely used. Now you can also automate follow-up with an email sequence on an auto responder, as well as personally with emails or phone calls, as appropriate.

- Using a website in this manner allows you to send people coming from different sources, for example, from your book, or from your social media, to land on different pages. When they optin to your email list, that page is recorded, and you can track who came from where – so now you know what marketing is working, and more importantly, ***which marketing is NOT working!***

TRANSFORMATION 9: LIST YOUR CURRENT ADVERTISING AND MARKETING TACTICS – for example, "flyer at tackshop," "flyer at feed store," or "<this> promoted post." Then note if/how you are tracking each.

Yes, make a list here:

1. _____   4. _____

   _____   _____

2. _____   5. _____

   _____   _____

3. _____   6. _____

   _____   _____

This is a very important Transformation Item. Don't just skip ahead to the next chapter.

NOTES:

_____

_____

_____

10

CLIENT VALUE

If you did the first 13 Transformations, congratulate yourself! You've just done lots more for yourself than most businesses EVER do to make life easy for themselves. <u>Award yourself a nice, big carrot!</u>

You didn't? Stop right now, go back to the Transformation, and do your homework! <u>No carrots for you until you do!</u>

<u>On the flip side is the less enjoyable, less profitable customer... and less enjoyable, less profitable activities</u>. Even before you have all the IDEAL customers you can serve, you can let these less profitable ones go... freeing up resources so you can better serve your IDEAL customer, making you more profitable, so you can let even more of the less profitable ones go... until you reach a happy balance point.

I know it sounds risky. "But these guys pay the bills!" I can hear you thinking. They might. But the cost is too much. Let's look at the drain on resources:

1. <u>Morale</u> – morale dips when you have clients that aren't passionate, aren't teachable, aren't going to go home and practice what they learned. These are psychographic traits that you might look for in your Ideal clients.
2. Time – you, or your office personnel spend more time with the DUD client, finagling payments, arrangements, or whatever, than with the

IDEAL clients. This means you're spending more (time=money) on a less-than-ideal client than on your IDEAL. That's just wrong, isn't it?

<u>Why do you have DUD customers?</u>

Because you don't know how to get (and keep) the IDEAL ones. This can also be a symptom of not knowing what your ideal client is; of not having a system, or it might be a symptom of low self-esteem on your part.

All of these are easily remedied:

- Identifying even just a few IDEAL CLIENT traits to start with
- Systematizing lead generation
- Doing some self-esteem/confidence building work – it's actually easier than you might think.

Transformation 10: Customer Value

First we look at the value of different segments of your customers. Most businesses don't have any idea how much value (profit) their customer brings to their business.

So first we look at AVERAGE customer value. Then we'll look at your IDEAL customers and then at your DUD customers.

Average Customer Value

Then segment your clients into BEST and DUD clients, and do it again. If you don't have actual figures, do a best-guess. What are your:

- Average Customer Value (/yr):_____
- Average Lifetime Customer Value:_____
- IDEAL Client Value:_____
- IDEAL Client Lifetime Value:_____
- DUD Client Value:_____
- DUD CLV:_____

10.A.: Average Client Value: This takes your yearly profit, and divides it by the full number of clients you serviced (yes, write right in the book):

10.B: IDEAL Client Value: Now look at only your ideal clients, which may take a bit more work. Figure up your yearly profits from just THEM, and divide by the number of IDEAL clients.

10.C: DUD Client Value: This is calculated from those on your "DUD" list. . Looking at ONLY your DUD clients (full list minus Ideal or Best clients), figure up your yearly profits, and divide by the number of DUD clients.

<u>Lifetime Client Value</u> – This is a VERY important Transformation Item, one that absolutely should not be skipped or skimped on.

<u>Life time</u>: How long does your client work with you? While there are some industry averages, you really have to look at your own numbers. This is a BENCHMARK number, one by which you will judge your progress. It may also be a defining value for your IDEAL and DUD clients, so it REALLY behooves you to look at your clients over the lifetime of your business, and figure out how long each stayed with you.

Note: Lifetimes may be measured in weeks, months or years. You'll have to see what your lowest measurement is. I have assumed "years" for the calculation, but yours may be measured in weeks or months.

<u>$/yr</u> : How much profit do they bring to your business yearly (or other time increment)?

10.D: <u>AVERAGE Client Lifetime Value:</u>

10.E: <u>IDEAL Client Lifetime Value</u>

10.F: <u>DUD Client Lifetime Value</u>

What do these numbers tell you? Here are some things they might tell you:

- How much you can spend to GET each into your operation;
- How much you can spend to KEEP each in your operation;
- Which you want MORE of, which you want FEWER of.

When you can OUTSPEND your competition to GET and KEEP clients, you'll attract and keep better clients – but you <u>*HAVE*</u> to know how valuable they are to begin with, or you'll find yourself operating at a loss.

10.G: <u>Personal Hourly Value</u> This is an important number to track. The more you outsource lower-revenue-value work, the more you raise your personal hourly value, because now you focus on the more profitable, revenue-producing work.

<u>What does this number tell you?</u>

- What work you SHOULD do – and which you should outsource. Work that has less value than your hourly rate can be outsourced. You should be doing work that has higher per hour value.
- It gives you a starting point for determining your day rate.
- It gives you a point of reference to let you know if your operation is more or *less* profitable for you PERSONALLY.
- As you ADD more IDEAL clients, and CULL the DUDs, it goes up.

Whew! Did you make it through all that?

Yes, it's a LOT of work – but these numbers are critical to your business. And these are not numbers your accountant will ever generate for you – unless you specifically direct him to (and then he'll probably grumble about it, too).

- When you know your numbers, you know what you can or cannot spend on marketing, regardless of whether that is client acquisition or herd retention.

- When you know your numbers, you know if you are working for less than minimum... or if you are actually creating wealth.

When you know what your numbers mean, you can better define IDEAL clients, cull the DUDs, freeing up resources for the IDEAL clients... and for yourself.

And that's the first real step on the path to wealth and freedom.

NOTES:

11

Social Proof/Credibility

If you did the first 20 Transformations, congratulate yourself! You've just done lots more for yourself than most businesses EVER do to make life easy for themselves. **Award yourself a nice, big carrot!**

You didn't? Stop right now, go back to the Transformation, and do your homework! **No carrots for you until you do!**

"Everybody knows..." What does "everybody know" about you? What benefit can others' experience in working with you bring to your business? And what is this "social proof" thing all about anyway?

First questions first – What IS social proof?

Social proof is the old concept of "safety in numbers." It shows us (the unconverted crowd) the experience others have had.

3 Kinds of Social Proof

There are at least 3 kinds of social proof:

1. Proof that the concept of what you are doing/teaching is valid.
2. Proof that YOU get RESULTS.
3. Proof that YOU are a great person.

Let's go through each of these.

1. **Proof of concept.**

    Example: When I started marketing my book-writing, I didn't have any clients, and no testimonials. So I used the examples of OTHER people that my target audience would recognize to show that this was a legitimate marketing strategy.

    I used the examples of Dan Kennedy, the marketing consultant, coach and guru; Frank Kern, Jeff Walker, Robert Kiyosaki, and Jane Savoie.

    There may have been better examples, but these came to mind, they had all used books in at least some of their marketing (Dan Kennedy uses books extensively in the early stages of his marketing), and there was enough range that both my internet marketing friends and my equestrian friends would find somebody familiar.

    I also use a powerful quote from Jay Conrad Levinson, the late Author of the Guerilla Marketing series.

    =>This could involve the subjects' quotes, any published case studies you might find, or you might create your own mini-case studies.

2. **Proof of results.**

    Of course, this is always the best kind of social proof. If you have a client that can stand up and say "I increased my [x] by [y%] and that resulted in [highly desired result] without [highly undesirable problem]," that is always best.

    You get these after you have clients.

    Certainly if you have somebody who's any sort of celebrity as a client, you should approach them for their testimonial. As they are recognized, at least within certain groups, it becomes an endorsement, not just a testimonial.

Endorsements are most often used in books, but of course can be attached to anything. For example, because Brittany Spears used and got results from ProActive™, and because she is a celebrity, her testimonial is a powerful endorsement.

That's why having a system for getting and using really useful testimonials is HIGHLY recommended – and why I do that for clients.

3. **Personal proof**

This is when people say "[Your Name] really looks out for your best interests" or whatever other appropriate remarks that are about you personally.

It's useful, although not as useful in most selling situations as the result-proof. Most "testimonials" that are offered really fall into this category.

Again, that's why having an organized system is so valuable. You can collect testimonials that allow you to overcome objections in a sales setting, which then allows you to sell more, sell at higher price points, and to sell more frequently (depending on your product and market, of course).

Why do you NEED social proof?
You need social proof if you want to be recognized as the expert you are. We're not talking about BECOMING the expert – we're talking about demonstrating your expertise to prospects, people who don't know that you're as good as you are in [whatever you do].

So if you want to be accepted as an expert, you need credibility. You need a demonstration of that expertise, and you **need** others to recognize it.

When we meet this condition, we no longer have the "Why is that flake down the road able to charge so much more than I can when she's not even 10% as good as I am!" conversation.

She's *demonstrated.* You *haven't.* She may also be a better salesperson than you.

The good news is that this is a fixable problem.

How do you GET Social Proof (Credibility)?
You demonstrate. You ask for proof. You USE.

So if you are a riding instructor, you ask your clients for feedback on individual sessions, but you also have them test at various things to demonstrate that they are learning/improving. In various jumping disciplines, this is often a height measurement. In dressage, it might be progressing to new movements, tests, or levels.

So you would run the student through a test, remind them how they were doing [a month, 6 months, whatever time frame] ago, and ask them how they feel about their progress.

You could record their reaction right in the riding school. Then you ask them several specific questions, which you record, make sure you have permission to use this, and send it off to your assistant to upload, get transcribed, and use in various things, such as:

- The farm's YouTube Channel, Instagram, Facebook, Twitter, Tumblr, and other social media.
- Your monthly newsletter.
- Your website.
- Your display at events.
- Your book, and so forth.

Or maybe you have a tack/feed store. Hold an event, where people will actually come in, do something amazing for them, and then ask them several specific questions that will bring out great testimonials.

What are these questions I should ask?

The best, awesomely-useful-testimonial-getting questions I've ever seen are on the CopyBlogger.com site.

---

6 Questions To Ask For Powerful Testimonials, by Sean d'Souza

https://www.copyblogger.com/testimonials-part-2/

These are questions I revisit every time I start a new project – as naturally, each project must have it's own testimonial-gathering-setup.

How do I actually go about gathering these testimonials?

We're going to assume a few things:

1. You have clients or customers of some sort.
2. You do good enough work to make your clients/customers [whatever term you use to describe them] happy.

So the next step is to set up a system, as simple or as complex as required, to gather the testimonials.

We already have part 1 – the happy clients, and part 2 – the basic questions. Typically, I modify the questions a bit to fit the situation.

So now, we have to figure out how to get the happy client in front of the question. Here's my typical strategy:

- **If there are lots of people, set up an automated system**. I might set up the questions on a Google Drive Form, then use an email, a chatbot, or some other mass communication channel, to send them to the form. Set it up in advance, with multiple ways to get them there – a button on the website thank-you page; an email in your autoresponder sequence, and a chatbot message in your followup sequence.
- **If you work more with higher-ticket buyers**, you might include it on your checklist, and even get on cam with them to ask the questions in person, interview-style.
- **In the end, it doesn't matter HOW you do it – just THAT you do it**. I've included suggestions at the end of the book on

Now you need to USE the testimonial. Here is a non-inclusive list of ways to use testimonials:

- On social media. Hand them off to your Social Media Manager. She'll use them on all your social networks.
- On your website. Use them on a dedicated testimonials page, targeted places (and testimonials) on your sales pages, in your online presentations, etc.
- On your brochures and other print media.
- In your book – and if you have enough, publish a separate book just for them.
- In your advertising. Many times, it's better to have somebody else talk about you than it is for YOU to talk about you.
- On a display at an expo. Have only a few? Display all of them. Have a ton? Again, dedicate a display to as many as you can fit into it.
- Here are some other suggestions, on page 93. There is also a SAMPLE agreement for you to use on page 97.

Transformation #21-25: Take steps to start collecting social proof.

- **"Starting today,** I [YOUR NAME HERE], have decided to collect social proof." _____Signature
_____ Date
- **How many clients** do you currently have? #_____
- **What forms of media** do they use (check all that apply):
  - Mobile device:_____
  - Email: _____
  - Camera:_____
  - Desktop computer:_____
- **Check Appendix ()** for a sample permission-to-use-likeness-and-name form. Seriously consider including this in all new-client-intake, orientation, or setup forms.
- **LOOK at the questions on CopyBlogger.com** at https://www.copyblogger.com/testimonials-part-2/. **Connect** with me if you'd like help 'massaging' them to fit your situation.
  - Q#1: _____
  _____
  - Q#2: _____
  _____
  - Q#3: _____
  _____
  - Q#4: _____
  _____
  - Q#5: _____
  _____
  - Q#6: _____
  _____

NOTES: _____
_____
_____
_____

12

REFERRAL SYSTEMS

If you did the first 25 Transformations, congratulate yourself! You've just done lots more for yourself than most businesses EVER do to make life easy for themselves. <u>Award yourself a nice, big carrot!</u>

You didn't? Stop right now, go back to the Transformation, and do your homework! <u>No carrots for you until you do!</u>

Referrals are the BEST way to get (and keep) clients. Do you use them, and if you do, do you have a system for ensuring that you get them, or is it hit-or-miss?

> *"One customer, well taken care of, could be more valuable than $10,000 worth of advertising."*
>
> — *Jim Rohn*

Of course, that depends on the business – but how much does it cost you to get a client? How much does it cost you to keep them?

- The Word of Mouth Marketing Association reports that every day in the United States, there are approximately 2.4 billion brand-related conversations. People frequently talk about the products and services they enjoy, and the companies who offer them.

- 92% of consumers trust referrals from people they know – **Nielsen**[2]
- People are 4 times more likely to buy when referred by a friend – **Nielsen**[3]
- 77% of consumers are more likely to buy a new product when learning about it from friends or family. – **Nielsen**[4]
- 81% of U.S. online consumers' purchase decisions are influenced by their friends' social media posts versus 78% who are influenced by the posts of the brands they follow on social media. – **Market Force**[5]
- 43% of consumers are more likely to buy a new product when learning about it from friends on social media. – **Nielsen**[6]
- 85% of fans of brands on Facebook recommend brands to others. – **Syncapse**[7]
- 84% of consumers say they either completely or somewhat trust recommendations from family, colleagues, and friends about products – making these recommendations the information source ranked highest for trustworthiness. – **Nielsen**[8]
- 74% of consumers identify word-of-mouth as a key influencer in their purchasing decision. – **Ogilvy/Google/TNS**[9]
- 1 offline word of mouth impression drives sales at least 5x more than 1 paid, and much more (as much as 100 times more) for higher-consideration categories. – **WOMMA**[10]
- Word of mouth is the primary factor behind 20% to 50% of all purchasing decisions. – **McKinsey**[11]

---

[2] **Nielsen** –
[3] **Nielsen** -
[4] **Nielsen** -
[5] **Market Force** -
[6] **Nielsen** -
[7] **Syncapse** -
[8] **Nielsen** -
[9] **Ogilvy/Google/TNS** -
[10] **WOMMA** -
[11] **McKinsey** -

- 49% of U.S. consumers say friends and family are their top sources of brand awareness.
- 71% of consumers are more likely to make a purchase based on social media referrals.
- On social media, 58% of consumers share their positive experiences with a company, and ask family, colleagues, and friends for their opinions about brands. [**SDL**][12]
- Consumers rely on word-of-mouth 2x to 10x more than paid media. – **Boston Consulting Group**[13]
- 55% of consumers share their purchases socially on Facebook, Twitter, Pinterest and other social sites.
- 59% of Pinterest users have purchased an item they saw on the site, 33% of Facebook users have purchased an item they saw on their news feed or a friend's wall.
- Word-of-mouth has been shown to improve marketing effectiveness by up to 54%. – **MarketShare**[14]

So as you can easily see, referrals are easily the best (and the least expensive) marketing method.

There are other benefits too.

- Referral Marketing generates 3-5x higher conversion rates than any other channel.
- The lifetime value of a new referral customer is 16% higher than your average customer. – **Wharton School of Business**[15]
- The Lifetime Value of a referred customer is 25% higher than that of other customers – **Wharton School of Business**[16]

---

[12] **SDL** -
[13] **Boston Consulting Group** -
[14] **MarketShare** -
[15] **Wharton School of Business** -
[16] **Wharton School of Business** -

- When specific case studies about referral software were analyzed, researchers found a 10% increase in WOM (off and online) translated into a sales lifts between 0.2 – 1.5%. – **MarketShare/ Keller Fay Group**[17]
- Referred customers bring you 25% higher profit margin.
- A referred customer is 18% more loyal than a customer acquired by other means.
- Referred customers are 4 times more likely to refer more customers to your brand.
- Customers referred by other customers have a 37% higher customer retention rate.
- Customer acquisitions through referrals spend 200% more than the average customer.
- Robust advocacy-marketing programs are achieving significant revenue gains—10 to 20 percent for established products and up to 100 percent for new products.

And best of all – when a current client MAKES a referral, they are much more likely to STAY with you – and they spend more with you too.

So how do you GET that referral?

You need a system.

1. **Deliver.** First off, deliver a great experience. You've probably been in the situation of referring somebody to a resource, and if that resource isn't up to par, you are NOT going to refer them to it. So first and foremost, make sure you're up to par.
2. **Ask-Ask-Ask.** Ask your clients. I tell my clients that I'm going to ask them for referrals even before I take them on. It's part of the requirement for working with me. So they are expecting it. Ask them on a regular basis... but not before you...
3. **Give them a way to make that referral.** Some things are easy to refer. You have a student who did well at a show, they will talk about it,

---

[17] **MarketShare/ Keller Fay Group** -

naturally, and their friends will naturally ask who they train with. In other cases, it's not so easy. That's when you want to make it easy for them. This might include giving them anything from a packet of business cards for them to share with friends/associates, or it might include a whole package – a referral letter, a dvd, a book, a few newsletters, depending on your business and the client value – that they simply hand off to the referral.

4. **A promise that you'll take great care of the referral –** even if they don't come on as a client. BE sure you actually do this – trust damaged is really hard to rebuild.

5. **Potentially, you might also have a reward system in place.** Again, this depends on what you sell, how you sell it, and the client value. Incentivizing can definitely work.

Almost all businesses say they get referrals "because we are so awesome." 79% don't have a system in place, and therefore the few they do get are few and far between.

Having a REAL system in place – and it doesn't have to be super complicated, it just needs to be useable – makes consistent referrals a reality. It also takes you from being "in business" to being a REAL BUSINESS.

Transformation 26:

1. Do you currently have a system of getting referral business on a consistent basis? _____

2. What is one way that you can help your current clients/customers /patients or members refer other people to you? _____

3. What do those referrals need to know in order to become a client?
   a. _____
   b. _____
   c. _____

13

PERFECT MARKETING

If you did the first 26 Transformations, congratulate yourself! You've just done lots more for yourself than most businesses EVER do to make life easy for themselves. **<u>Award yourself a nice, big carrot!</u>**

You didn't? Stop right now, go back to the Transformation, and do your homework! **<u>No carrots for you until you do!</u>**

In a perfect world, there is no competition. Do you believe that?

I don't.

In a perfect world, we *require* competition. We need it to hone our individuality, to create new and exciting products, services, and understanding.

Competition forces you to hone your craft, to hone your marketing, to specialize, to become better in some regard, to some market, during some space of time.

I LOVE competition.

In a perfect world, nobody could ever copy your marketing. It is, however, quite possible to copy a book, and, with some work, even a complete website. While the odds of it happening are extremely slim, it's not unheard of.

Sending a **Digital Millennium Copyright Act**[18] (DMCA) take-down notification to the web hosting provider removes a copied website.

Yes, they'll be upset – but then they DIDN'T take advantage of my exclusive offer and guarantee to you.

Getting a copied book removed is a little more complicated. If a knocked-off-appearing book appears in your market, grab a copy of it and send it along to me. I'll help you verify that it's really and truly a knock off. If it is, that is also a copyright infringement issue, and may involve your attorney. Again, that's likely solved with a DMCA take-down notice.

"Me-Too Marketing" – what we call it when somebody copies us – misses more than a few of the under-the-cover pieces we put into place, and is therefore much, much less effective.

<u>**The big picture is that we are using a full-blown strategy, not just a few scattered tactics to complement current marketing, and to build your full-blown marketing strategy.**</u> So many things go into crafting our strategy that it isn't something that can just be "knocked off."

Just like an iceberg that shows only 10% of its mass above the waterline, so what the uneducated eye sees of your marketing only "shows" about 10% of what is going on.

Even if a competitor actually knows what is going on behind the scenes, they can't copy it – it would be individual and customized to them, not copied from you. So ironically, if they copy you, they do their own drilling down into their

---

[18] Digital Millennium Copyright Act, see more at
http://en.wikipedia.org/wiki/Digital_Millennium_Copyright_Act

IDEAL client, they end up creating their own business-specific marketing, and in so doing, don't and can't ever directly copy you.

PLUS – I give you 18 strategies later on in this book that you can use with in conjunction with your own book to exponentially leverage your investment, and to multiply your presence, authority and celebrity status in your community – and especially in regards to your target market.

Some of these are things that you will personally do. Some of them are things that are best left to a professional. Some of them are so much work and so complicated, that most people simply throw their hands up in despair and won't do them.

But as you know, the difference between somebody who's a huge success, and one who isn't, is often the sheer volume or the degree of detail of what they are willing to do. Complicated is good. It works for us.

In a nutshell: your marketing won't be knocked off.

NOTES:_____

_____

_____

_____

_____

_____

_____

_____

14

HOW TO MAKE BEST USE OF YOUR MARKETING $$

If you've done the Transformations in the previous chapters, you've laid the groundwork for a deeper marketing strategy. You've also done a lot more work than most businesses, large OR small, EVER do to understand their market and to hone their activities to bring in better customers.

Here are some ways to make the best use of your marketing resources:

1. **Make *all* marketing accountable**. Know where all segments of clients come from. If marketing doesn't pull, kill it. If you can't find SOME way of tracking it, don't use it. Advertising salespeople have (1) motive – to sell more advertising. They don't REALLY care, much less even know, if it's truly effective for you. Remember that – especially when they say things like "you need repetition" or that a client needs to hear your message X-# of times before they act. If your IDEAL client hears/sees your well-crafted message, they will respond. NOW.

2. **KNOW who you are trying to reach.** Build a profile of your IDEAL client. Build disqualifiers into your marketing, so unfit candidates disqualify themselves.

3. **Focus on the activities that are BOTH most personally enjoyable for you, AND which are most profitable**. Pick clients who use those, and cull those who don't. You'll enjoy your work more, you'll make more money, adding to the enjoyment; your clients, who are now getting better service, are happier, will stay with you longer and will spend more.

4. **Establish yourself as an authority and as a celebrity**. The best, and by far the easiest way to do this is to write the right book – and hook it into an appropriately-designed website. Juice those up with powerful marketing. This sets up an amazing marketing machine, pumping IDEAL clients into your business, and streamlining profits.

5. **Start NOW.** Do the Transformation exercises. Look for ways to make your current marketing accountable. Your competition may be complacent today, but tomorrow they may decide to take action. Beat them to the punch – take action today.

NOTES:

15

BONUS: 18 MARKETING STRATEGIES FOR USING A BOOK TO MASSIVELY GROW YOUR CLINICIAN, INSTRUCTION, OR COACHING BUSINESS

STRATEGY #1 – LOCAL MEDIA

The first strategy is to send media releases to your local and regional media outlets, including newspaper, radio stations, magazines, and T.V. Stations. A press release (or media release, as most like to call them) is an official communication to a media outlet to inform them of something specific. The GOAL of the media release is to do one or more of the following:

- *Get the media release published.*
- *Get somebody from that media to interview you*, write a story, which is then published to their readers, viewers or listeners.
- And/or *get the opportunity to be a contributor* to their media outlet.

In some cases, your media release might get published as-is, so you always want to end it with an invitation for readers to get a copy of your book – AND you always want to extend that invitation if you are actually interviewed too.

If you are invited to come on board as a contributor, you can use your book as content to publish in your column or a newsletter, so you don't even have to do any actual writing. *The BIG benefit here is you have the added credibility of using "John Doe, Author, and Contributor to (name of newspaper/TV station/Radio station/magazine)."*

NOTES:_____

_____

_____

_____

_____

STRATEGY #2 – NATIONAL MEDIA

You can use your book to get on national media such as ABC, NBC, CNN, FOX, Wall Street Journal, and others. As you are an equestrian[19] clinician, that includes the national/international horse-related magazines.

Once you've gotten on those national media, you'll add something that says "Author, As Seen on (whichever outlet)" to your business card, your website, your brochures – all of your marketing collateral.

AND of course, once you do that, you share it on all your social media profiles, websites, email newsletters, and any other place you communicate with your target market.

Think for just a moment about how using just these 2 marketing strategies will differentiate you from your competition. What did we just do?

We:

1. *Created a marketing piece* (the book) that we then leveraged first
2. LOCALLY. Media LOVES books, and especially loves local authors, so it's a safe bet it gets picked up locally and regionally;

---

[19] "Equestrian in the broad sense of the term, meaning somebody who works with horses, rather than just meaning "one who rides a horse".

3. *Then we took it national.* How many of your local competitors can say they've been on ABC or CNBC or CNN? That's right – not many of them.
4. Then we *got copies of those publications or broadcasts*, and we leveraged *that*, by making sure that both current clients and prospective ones, can read, see or hear this broadcast. AND there are other tricks one can do to leverage a tv appearance, which I share with my clients:

   For example: have a small crew do a "behind the scenes" shoot of you ON the set, and you share that everywhere and at every opportunity too.

Do you see how powerful this all is? If your target market knows about you, and your celebrity and authority status, that gives you a definitive edge over your competitors.

Let's look at this from the perspective of your potential client. If you are in the market looking for somebody to instruct you, to train your horse, to show your horse – whatever it is you do – would you go with somebody who's an author and has been on all these media platforms, or would you go with a nobody that hasn't?

NOTES:_____

_____

_____

_____

_____

_____

_____

STRATEGY #3 – LOCAL, REGIONAL, & NATIONAL HORSE ASSOCIATIONS

As horse business people and aficionados, we all belong to any number of horse-related associations. So do your target market – your IDEAL clients. Wouldn't it be amazing if those associations were to assist you in actually marketing your business?

I mean, beyond the member listing they so graciously give you as a paid member. And I also mean beyond the paid listings, or the sponsorship-granted marketing opportunities. What if you could do something so awesome that they would actually talk about you?

Writing your book is your first step. Getting it mentioned in local and regional media is the next step. Now you're going to send a few copies of your book, along with your very targeted media release, written specifically for each association, and copies of your locally and regionally garnered press.

Here's what you're looking for here:

- Perhaps they *just publish the press release*, which like all the others, invites the reader to your site for more info.
- Perhaps a bespoke *write up of the book*.
- *An interview* which they write up, or publish the audio or video of on their website.
- And again, perhaps the opportunity to contribute to their publications.
- They may even like you so much that they find a way to sponsor you.

Again, this can be as targeted as you like – do you know how many thousands of horse associations, societies, clubs and whatnot there are in the United States alone? Thousands.

This just got interesting, didn't it?

NOTES:_____

_____

_____

Strategy #4 – Regional, National, & Activity Specific Magazines

How many horse publications are you aware of? While there are hundreds of nationally/internationally distributed magazines, there are nearly as many regional ones. And they are all looking for material to publish.

Some of these magazines are more targeted to your IDEAL client than others, so you MAY want to make a list of which ones to send to, depending on your:

- Location
- Geographic scope – are you a local, regional or nationally based company?
- Specialty – if you teach dressage, you want to target riders looking for dressage instruction, for example. While there are a few barrel racers who understand that dressage helps them ride better, most won't. Conversely, if you teach barrel racing, very few dressage riders will ever be interested.

So you'll send your packet of your book, your release, your interview questions, and any other materials you may have to your list of regional and national magazines.

Again, you're looking for them to:

- Get the media release published.
- Get somebody from that media to interview you, write a story, which is then published to their readers, viewers or listeners.
- And/or get the opportunity to be a contributor to their media outlet.

Now this really differentiates you from your competitors, doesn't it?

NOTES:_____

_____

_____

_____

_____

STRATEGY #5 – MAIL

Your business has geographic constraints. Your clients, IDEAL or otherwise will only drive so far in order to get to you. There is a limit, isn't there? If you hold clinics, that limit may be extended out to several hours – but they only come on an infrequent basis.

For regular instruction, people typically come from within a 30-45 minute drive.

So for a marketing strategy to reach those people, it's more efficient for them to come to you.

But here's how we can go to THEM.

We can mail your book to every address in a specific radius of your facility. As horse people are usually only a fraction of the population, that's still rather inefficient, so we can do the following two steps:

1. *We look at your IDEAL client's demographics*, pulling out characteristics that we can use to narrow down the list – rather than simply mailing to everybody in that specific radius, we're now mailing to affluent communities, people who've registered specific kinds of vehicles, etc.
2. *We can then take that list, and mail a copy of the book to each*, inviting them to visit your website, book an appointment, or to call a free recorded message – whatever action we decide we'd like them to take.

So is it useful to set geographic parameters or focus for your business? Is it useful to target people of certain demographics, such as age, income, business owner or employee, homeowner or renter, owner of specific vehicles – such as a horse trailer?

If so, we can use this book mailing method to get in front of them.

Before you dismiss the idea of a mailing or say "Mail doesn't work," it's important to remember that when it comes to advertising or marketing, the success or failure of the effort to increase your sales is NOT THE RESULT of the media that you use.

If you tried social media, for example, and it didn't work, it isn't the fault of the social media site that you used.

If you tried an advertisement, or a flyer, and it didn't work, it isn't the advertisement or the flyer's fault. If you tried direct mail, and it didn't work, it isn't the fault of the post office, the mailman, or the mailing piece.

The problem lies with WHO you are attempting to sell to – and the MESSAGE you got in front of them.

When most business people think about increasing sales, the first thing they think is "Let's put an advert in the paper."

This is 100%, completely and totally, utterly wrong. You are literally putting the cart before the horse (although I've seen a picture where that worked).

The VERY first thing you MUST do is figure out EXACTLY *who* you want to talk to, and then *what* you'll say to them.

For example: think of a $1 bill and a $100 bill. Isn't the difference in value the message that's on the paper – NOT the paper itself? When advertising efforts don't work, it's usually not the fault of the ad. It's typically a problem with matching your message to your market.

NOTES:_____

_____

STRATEGY #6 – LEAD GENERATION

Another good option with using Direct Mail, instead of simply mailing your book to even a targeted list in a given market area, is to mail out a postcard or letter inviting people to call your office (or visit your website, or call a free recorded message) and request a copy of your book.

When they request it, ask for their name, email, mailing address, and phone number. Ask them how interested they are in what you offer, and their time frame for the services or products that meet the need that you fill.

You now have what is called a LEAD – somebody who is interested in your information, and in your business.

This can also be done via a magazine ad, a newspaper ad, a radio ad, a billboard ad – or any other media. *HAVE a way and a reason for people to respond to your advertising.*

Pro's Tip: If you use advertising strategies to generate leads, I highly recommend having a tracking phone number. This is a phone number that automatically forwards calls to your office phone. At the end of each day/week/month, you get a report that says X calls came from ad #1, and Y calls came from ad #2. You can determine which ad pulls better, stop spending money on places/ads that don't work as well, and reallocate those marketing dollars to more of the ads that DO pull well.

NOTES:_____

STRATEGY #7 – INCENTIVIZE INITIAL APPOINTMENTS

If you are getting enough leads, but have difficulty getting appointments for clinics, use the book as a way to get that appointment. You could send them the book when they set an appointment, or you can give it to them when they actually show for the appointment. *This is EXTREMELY useful, and very underused.*

NOTES:_____

STRATEGY #8 – FOLLOW UP WITH UNCONVERTED PROSPECTS

If you generate leads and you get appointments, but not the sale, a book is a GREAT reason to follow up with those leads you already have now.

Using your book to convert a bank of unconverted leads can repay your investment for the entire program in a very short period of time. Call your leads and offer them the book as a thank you for (whatever action we want them to take). Make sure it's autographed.

NOTES:_____

STRATEGY #9 – GIVE AS A "THANK YOU" GIFT

Use your book as a Thank You gift at ANY stage of your marketing process. Thank You for calling, Thank You for setting an appointment, Thank You for keeping your appointment, Thank You for participating in a clinic, or for setting one up; Thank You for signing up with us, Thank You for your business, Thank You for referring..

And of course you should autograph it, which makes it so much more special for the recipient!

NOTES:_____

STRATEGY #10 – CAPTURE LEADS ON WEBSITE

One thing that I've noticed in my many years online is that many business owners are concerned with their ranking in the search engines. They want to be #1 for their keywords – which is natural. What's baffling that once I get to the website, I'm confused as to what they want me to do next.

What do you want people to DO on your site? Here's what I mean:

Let's say for a moment that I run a car dealership. Every day, people come into the business, they kinda look around, maybe they get into a car, they walk around a little bit, and then they leave.

It's madness to NOT send out a salesman. I want my salesmen talking to people who are looking at my cars.

Having a website that's well ranked is nearly completely useless unless you have a way to get a way to follow up with your visitors. That's why we get their name and email – so we can follow up with them over time, inviting them to become a customer.

And it's super easy when you have a book to offer a few chapters as an incentive to provide their contact info. In fact, if I met YOU at a networking event, a trade show, or if I sent you something in the mail, I invariably ask you for your email so I can send you follow up materials.

Let's go back to the car dealership example. I spent $1200 on advertising last week, and 12 people visit the store on Saturday. I've just paid $100 per visitor to bring them in. If I just let 11 of them walk out without buying anything, I have WASTED $1100. If only one person buys something, that means my "COST PER SALE" is $1200.

The list of things WRONG with that scenario is so long I could do a 2-day seminar on it. What could the car dealer owner do to cover his investment?

He could get each visitor's mailing and email address to send them coupons or sales announcements, or a bottle of leather cleaner or a pillow in the mail – it's not rocket science.

But so many clinicians make this same exact mistake online. They spend tons of time, money, and energy to get people to their site – but then fail to get names and emails and phone numbers of interested prospects.

So even if we DON'T end up working together, ask your webmaster about adding a lead capture system mechanism with a lead incentive and follow up system... but don't be too surprised if he has no clue what any of that is, much less how to implement it

I'm passionate about this, and it pains me to no end to see honest business owners leaving so much money on the table, and/or wasting money when it really isn't necessary.

And it's unethical for people who sell advertising or media who can't or won't measure the results.

If we work together, not only do I do ALL this exciting and cool book stuff and media publicity for you, BUT we also measure the results that it brings in. You'll know the exact dollar amount it brings in.

There is no "spray and pray" marketing, no Hope Marketing here, where you cross your fingers and hope it works.

It's scientific, tracked, measured and proven. You'll see dollar-for-dollar your exact results when I handle any aspect of marketing for you.

NOTES:_____

_____

_____

_____

_____

_____

STRATEGY #11 – SEND IT AS A GIFT

If a client or a prospect doesn't already have your book, give it to them as a gift for a birthday, anniversary, a thank you, or as congratulations.

This is a great thing to do if you ever sponsor classes at shows or competitions, if you hold clinics at your facility, with other clinicians or you yourself: you can use the book to help drive registrations and/or attendance. If you want to use it to drive registrations, you send it out with their attendance information, after they have registered for the clinic. If you want it to drive attendance, to ensure people actually COME to the clinic, they get it when they check in.

Using it as a gift in a sponsored class is a little different. You might decide to hand it out to only those who place in the class, or you might choose to award it to everybody in the class. You'll want to make sure you bring enough to the show if you're going to give it to everybody in a class, and you may need help handing them out to class entrants, but it would make a HUGE impression on your target market to do it this way.

You want to be extremely selective about the class you sponsor, if you're going to hand them out to everybody, as you want to very carefully target your IDEAL client.

Either way, autographing it makes it ever so much more valuable to recipients. You can also use autographing a book as a means to build a bit of viral networking buzz – here's how.

Let's say I'm at a horse show or a trade event, like an expo, and Mary has just asked me for my autograph in a book I've just handed her for free. I've already gotten her business card if she has one. I'm always thrilled to autograph a book, so I intentionally DO NOT bring a pen to the conversation – I turn to John, who's standing nearby, in conversation with Susy, and I ask HIM for a pen.

Now John and Susy both want a book, and pretty soon a crowd gathers around, as I sign books, hand pens back (hopefully to the right owner) and borrow more, to sign a book for somebody else.

Just be sure to bring enough books! If you run out of books, get the name, phone #, mailing and email addresses of people who still want them.

NOTES:_____

_____

_____

STRATEGY #12 – BUILD A PROMOTION

When your book is written correctly, it's a great tool for creating promotions. Giving away your book is easily tied to a holiday of your choice:

- New Year's
- Valentine's Day
- St. Patrick's Day
- April Fool's Day
- Memorial Day
- Father's Day

- Independence Day
- Back-To-School
- Labor Day
- Halloween
- Thanksgiving
- Christmas

Or any of many other holidays, recognition and awareness days. I can help you build any of these promotions ahead of time, so that it's ready to go.

NOTES:_____

_____

_____

_____

STRATEGY #13 – NETWORKING ON STEROIDS

This is a strategy that I've actually already talked about. It's a high-powered strategy, one that resulted in a friend getting an offer for a position as an adjunct professorship – at the ripe old age of 23.

Go to the networking event. Don't bring business cards, just copies of your book. Walk around, chat with people, and hand them out. It's very high impact, very, very impressive.

Then offer to sign the book. If I'm talking with Mary, give her the book, then offer to sign it. DO NOT BRING A PEN – so that you can ask somebody else nearby, John, if he has a pen, so that I can autograph my book for Mary. Then he wants one, then an interested crowd gathers around you, and everybody wants a book.

Really cool, for everybody involved, really fun. This is a really memorable way to network. OF COURSE you get their card in exchange for the book, and you FOLLOW UP to get the appointment.

If you run out of books, KEEP ONE BOOK. Instead of handing them the book at this point, ask for their card, and offer to email something to them, like a special report (I can help with creating that too). You can also mail a book or email a few chapters of the book too.

This strategy can be highly leveraged, so be careful with it! ;-)

NOTES:_____

_____

_____

_____

_____

_____

STRATEGY #14 – "MEET THE AUTHOR"

Stage and hold a "Meet the Author" event, perhaps in conjunction with an open house, at your facility, or before or after a clinic. You'll have a book signing where current and former clients and prospects come in for a free copy of your book, you sign it, and then you take a picture with them (their phone or yours). Post the pictures on your website, social media profiles, and you can have them share them as well.

You can even have the pictures printed up, framed, and given to them on the spot, or mailed a few days later.

This can also be further leveraged with strategies #1, #11, & #15

NOTES:_____

_____

_____

_____

_____

STRATEGY #15 – CREATE A SEMINAR

You're a clinician, so you already do this.

If you have the space to gather a number of people at one time, or if you can easily get one (it's super easy to get space at hotels, or even small local motels), invite your prospects to come and learn about what you do.

Offer a copy of your book for attending.

Also, be sure to record audio and video of your seminar event, which can be leveraged in the next strategy.

NOTES:_____

_____

_____

_____

_____

STRATEGY #16 – CREATE VIDEO OR AUDIO SEMINARS

An audio seminar can be VERY easily put together, using a conference phone line. This is called a teleseminar. I personally have years of experience in putting these on – I've done over 100 of them, and can help you do one if we work together.

Rather than ask people to get in their vehicle and schlep to a facility or a hotel or library conference room, we invite them using my tested and proven process to simply call a phone number and listen to the presentation.

You are on the phone live, and present information on how your business is different and better, or it can be pre-recorded. At the end, you invite them to call your office, visit your website to set up an appointment, or whatever specific offer you chose.

An Audio + Visual online seminar is sometimes called a webinar, and it's sort of like a video seminar. It can be done live, or it can be recorded into a long video that we put on your website, on YouTube (or both). People are highly visual learners, and they retain more information from a video presentation when they watch and learn about you, your business, your book, what differentiates you, and what's in it for them.

You can use this technology to reach prospects as well as current clients. These can be free or paid. It all depends on what your strategy is.

Your book can be the basis on any presentation, so you don't have to prep much. Plus, if we work together, I can assist in putting things together for this sort of presentation. And let me tell you, having a book to work from makes setting up a presentation about 1000x easier than doing one from scratch.

Then, after the presentation has been recorded, it can be duplicated onto DVDs or CDs, which of course I also am skilled at, and can assist with. You can then send these in the mail to new prospects, bundle them with your book, etc.

You WANT to do this because:

1. The book establishes your status and authority.

2. Some people prefer to read material, others prefer to LISTEN to it, and still others prefer to WATCH.

3. Having all three, especially if you bundle them together, gives you a VERY unique marketing strategy – one that I can just about guarantee won't be duplicated by ANYBODY.

Why is this so important? Why go to all this work and effort and attention to detail?

BECAUSE – the biggest question people have in their minds, ESPECIALLY those who might have been affected by the recent recession – is this:

Who Can I TRUST?

If you educate, motivate, and qualify your target market by educating them, by providing VALUE, without being pushy, they appreciate it, and feel the need to reciprocate.

They want to get to know YOU, in a no- or low-pressure situation, so that they KNOW if they fit well with you, the way you teach, train, and interact with them and their horses.

They want to make a good decision, especially when it concerns their riding career, and the well-being of their horse, so they want to go with the expert. Somebody who takes the time to educate them on HOW to properly MAKE the right decision is somebody they will work with.

That's why *I* wrote this book that you are reading right now. That's why you are considering writing your own.

We want people to listen to what we say before they run off and start talking to somebody else who doesn't know as much as we do about what we do best.

Yes, this does apply in our industry. I'm available for consultation to see how it applies to your specific situation – please visit page 63 to learn how to get a FREE consultation with me.

NOTES:_____

_____

_____

_____

_____

STRATEGY #17 – ONLINE MARKETING

In a fashion very similar to how we just took your book and turned it into an live seminar, an audio teleseminar, a webinar, put them online and on CDs and DVDs, your book content can very easily be used to create marketing content online for social media and search engine rankings.

Here are just a few of the many, many ways we can use your book online:

- Snippets of content posted on Facebook, Twitter, LinkedIn, Google+, and other social media profiles. Can be text, images, or short videos.
- Posting a piece of a chapter on your blog helps improve SEO, and the resulting improvement increases organic traffic to your site.
- Posting pieces of chapters of different blog sites such as WordPress.com, Blogspot, Tumbler, and many others.
- Create short videos or audio recordings and post them on video sites and podcast directories. You can easily have a series of videos on YouTube, Vimeo, Metacafe, and Daily Motion, all of which improve your search engine positions. Audio recordings can be posted on podcasts like iTunes and others.
- If you combine the book with strategies #1 and #2, you can announce your media presence on your social media profiles and your website, greatly compounding the effects of credibility and new traffic to your website, your book, and your business.

NOTES:_____

_____

_____

_____

_____

I've just handed you 17 great strategies for leveraging your new book. These are brilliant, highly leveraged marketing ideas that will generate new clients for you.

You don't have to use ALL of them, just using a few will more than pay for your writing and marketing packages.

But far-and-away, the single best strategy to using a book is to use it to get referrals... tons of referrals...

STRATEGY #18 – HOW TO USE YOUR BOOK TO GENERATE REFERRALS

Of course you already know what a referral is. Mary boards her horse at your facility, her friend Sarah is looking for a place, or is dissatisfied with where she is, or visits Mary and likes your facility, so arranges to move her horse there.

Referrals are the least costly way to get the best clients. It is also one of the least understood marketing strategies, and therefore one of the most underutilized ones.

So how do you leverage your new book to get your referral program hopping?

One of the best ways is to use it to create Offline Viral Marketing. You've heard of viral marketing – it's when Mary sees your video, shares it on her Facebook profile, then 10 of her friends see and love and share it, then 100 of theirs, and so on. It's a compounding, exponential exposure for your business.

In real life, it usually compounds only so far, then dies out. Some businesses live and die by it. For most, it's a lot of work, and it doesn't go as far as the model might indicate.

It can however, be somewhat replicated OFFLINE. You can indeed use the concept of viral marketing and word-of-mouth, and one of the easiest, best ways to start, is to give your book away to people who are "Centers of Influence." These are people who know and who are respected, by groups of people who are likely to use your facility's services.

This is called the "Offline Viral Marketing" strategy. Here's how it works:

1. *Identify a person* (or group) who has the friends, family, coworkers, peers, members, customers, clients, patients or network connections that you wish to serve.
2. *Give this person a number of copies of your book.* The number you give them depends on the size of their network. For example, if you wanted to reach a person's family members, you might give them 2 or 3 books. If they are a tack shop or feed store, you might leave a dozen or even a box of books, depending on the activity in the store, and their connection to the market.
3. *That center of influence gives away your books* to their family members or customers or members.
4. *THOSE people, in turn, connect with you* by phone or website or however you've chosen, so they can take the next step in becoming a client.

So first off, who can you GIVE those books to, so that they can pass them on to your target audience on your behalf?

- *Start with your current clients.* Give each current client at least 2-3 books, and specifically ask them to share them. "Here you are, Mary. I want you to have a copy of my new book. I also want you to have a few to share with friends or family that might also be interested in learning more. How many do you realistically think you need – how many friends do you have that are interested in dressage (or whatever your specialty is)?"
- *Tack and feed stores that service your geographic market area.* Make a list of relevant ones. If your specialty is dressage, for example, you *might*

not want to include a tack shop that sells ONLY western goods – as an example. That's a judgment call. Or you could test it, as when people call you, you should ask WHERE they got their book. Then you'll know which places to keep stocked in the future.

After making your list, call each, explaining that you're a new local equine author, and would they be willing to give a book to each customer – would their customers be interested in that. If you present it right, they might even be willing to do an email blast to their customer list, and invite them to come in and get a book for free (or even free with purchase)!

- *Local Horse Clubs, Groups, Associations, Societies*, etc, as relevant. Sometimes these are willing to work directly with you, just as I've described the tack and feed shops. Other times, they might be happier if you came and did a presentation, then offered your book for free to attendees. Groups that meet on a regular basis are often looking for presenters. Others, especially larger ones, realize they need to monetize their connection power, so they ask us to become a sponsor (pay them for the privilege).

- *Leverage the book to get speaking engagements.* As I mentioned above, many groups look for speakers. As you give your presentation, make references back to your book. At the end of the presentation, invite people to the back of the room, or to your booth, or where ever you've stashed your books, to come up and get an autographed copy. Get business cards from the "centers of influence" that you meet there, and leverage them to move up to bigger and bigger opportunities.

This Offline Viral Marketing strategy can be combined with all the other strategies we've discussed.

And, it's so effective because it combines expert status, authority positioning, and celebrity with an IMPLIED ENDORSEMENT of the tack shop, the local association, or whatever/whomever your center of influence is, which is very similar to what you get with referrals. It's really like taking a referral "fire" and dumping gallons of gasoline on it.

NOTES:_____

_____

_____

_____

_____

TRANSFORMATION 13: Referrals Strategy

1. Can you give your book to your current clients to generate referrals?
    a. YES _____
    b. NO_____
    c. MAYBE_____

2. Would these current clients take them?
    a. YES _____
    b. NO_____
    c. MAYBE_____

3. If they had extras, would they pass them on to friends, family, coworkers, peers, etc.?
    a. YES _____
    b. NO_____
    c. MAYBE_____

4. Are you a member of any networking groups (think horse associations, societies, clubs, etc), where you could donate your books, and/or offer an educational presentation or class on your service?
    a. _____
    b. _____
    c. _____

d. _____

5. Do you know of any businesses in your area that COULD refer to you but aren't currently? Where else serves the people you wish to reach?

   a. _____
   b. _____
   c. _____
   d. _____

6. Do you think that if you used your book, that you might get some of them to refer to you (give away your book, either for free, or as a gift-with-purchase)?

   a. YES _____
   b. NO_____
   c. MAYBE_____

7. Are there any centers of influence you'd LIKE to reach, but haven't been able to connect with?

   a. _____
   b. _____
   c. _____
   d. _____

8. Do you think that if you sent a FedEx package with your book, some testimonials, your CD or DVD, and a brief introductory letter that you might get some of them on the phone?

   a. YES _____
   b. NO_____
   c. MAYBE_____

NOTES:_____

_____

16

FREQUENTLY ASKED QUESTIONS

DIRECT RESPONSE MARKETING VS. "HOPE" MARKETING – HOW DO I KNOW WHAT I'M USING?

If you don't know, you're probably using "Hope Marketing." Direct Response Marketing entails a bit of education to implement, or, if you have somebody else setting up technical things for you, to understand the strategies and tactics. Understanding these things is more important than having the technical know-how to set them up. Tech can be hired. YOU NEED to understand WHY you are doing what you are doing.

The easy way to determine is to decide if your marketing efforts are more focused on:

- "Branding" yourself in the market, or on
- Getting a specific RESPONSE from the market, learning specifically WHICH marketing pulls and which does not, and using what works once you know.

It's your ship, your destiny. YOU need to be in control of it.

NOTES:_____

_____

_____

_____

_____

WHY DO "I" (OR MY BUSINESS) NEED A BOOK?

We use the properly-written book as an under-the-radar marketing piece to achieve these objectives:

1. Get your business – yourself – the publicity you WANT, but which you cannot get on your own.
2. Get the attention of your IDEAL client, and get them into your sales process. We set up the conversation so that they are chasing YOU, rather than you chasing THEM.
3. Indoctrinate new or current IDEAL clients, so they are fully aware of the full extent of your offering, and so they don't go over to a competitor.
4. You are established as the preeminent authority in your niche – the standard all others are judged by.

NOTES:_____

_____

_____

_____

_____

WHAT IS THE RIGHT WAY TO SET UP MY BOOK?

The RIGHT way to set up the book is to have somebody else do it. This is a sophisticated marketing piece, not a literary work or a biography or fiction – although a great many of THOSE are also "ghost written."

You need to focus on running your business – on giving riding lessons, training horses, competing horses for clients, keeping your stallion happy – whatever it is that you do best.

You DON'T want to do ALL the work of writing the book, and setting up the website – only to find out after investing hours of your precious time that you did it wrong, negating all the valuable time you spent working on the project and wasting both your time and money.

NOTES:_____

_____

_____

_____

_____

WHAT IS THE "RIGHT WAY" TO SET UP MY WEBSITE?

The RIGHT WAY to set up your website is to set it up as a forced-optin, direct response marketing machine, with an automatic followup email sequence. It forces people to get on your email list in order to see more. It automatically follows up with them to get them to take the actions you specify.

You MUST be selective here, to ask people to jump through hoops, because your book is sending highly qualified individuals to you; you WANT them to disqualify themselves, AND you have an "ethical bribe" behind that optin gate.

If people are visiting the site in order to GET your book, we'll have an option for them as well.

NOTES:_____

_____

_____

_____

How Can a Book "Fence In" My Herd (clients)?

Here are three ways in which your book will protect your clients from poaching by a competitor:

- **First, it programs current clients** to look at your competition in a new light, from a new perspective... the perspective YOU want them to use. Reading is a wonderful way to program (or reprogram) our minds, or those of our clients. You can literally program your IDEAL Client to STAY at your facility. It's a great way to reinforce the fences you have around your herd.
- **Second, you can easily use it to get prospects to qualify** or disqualify themselves, making your job much easier. The more IDEAL clients you have, the fewer total clients you even need.
- **Third, use your book to indoctrinate new clients**, to ensure they are getting the most out of working with you, that you have less corrective work to do to get them on track, on board, and running smoothly in their new "horse home."

In short, it protects your business, automates your customer retention and lead-generation work, and is a great "client orientation" tool, leading to greater customer retention.

NOTES:_____

_____

_____

_____

_____

How do I get word out about my new book?

In the last chapter, I gave you 18 different strategies to use to get your book out. Pick one and go with it. Then leverage it with some others.

Depending on the package you decide on, I can help you connect with your regular clients and even new clients via email, postal mail, and social media.

We'll work together with your local, regional and national media, bookstores, feed and tackshops to set up interviews with media, books and signing events in those places, as well as possibly set up an event at your facility.

You'll want to hand them out (or sell them) at events like expos, horse shows, and the like, using it like a business card. Use the strategies I gave you in the last chapter to ramp up how well that works for you.

We can also set up your site so people can order your new book from it, and connect back with you after they've read the book.

You can – and SHOULD – use it to magnify and amp up your current marketing. Your book is a GREAT leverage point to use with your current marketing strategies.

NOTES:_____

_____

_____

_____

_____

WHY SHOULD I LET YOU DO IT FOR ME INSTEAD OF A GHOSTWRITER I KNOW?

Because your ghostwriter friend might be a good writer... but they likely aren't good at direct response marketing. Or, more likely, even any marketing at all. They are just writers. That is all they do. Beyond crafting a highly specialized marketing piece, we are crafting a highly specialized

<u>marketing strategy</u> - not just an instructional book. You need somebody who knows what to write to get your reader to take the actions you desire, and then to further funnel and move them along your sales path.

<u>Because I do it the right way, the first time</u>. There is sooo much going on under the hood of this thing, that even I only trust people I PERSONALLY KNOW are expert Direct Response Marketers in specific specialties to even consider thinking about doing this on their own.. and even then, 90% of them will get a lot of it wrong.

<u>Because YOU need to focus on running your business, not on building new marketing pieces for it.</u> And certainly nothing as complicated as this machine is to get all up and running.

<u>Because I'm experienced at this</u>. I've been around the block, I've been there, done that. And for the technical pieces I'm not so personally good at, I have a crack team ready to jump in and do their amazing stuff. Rule #1 is always "Do What You Do BEST." That's why you have a farrier, a vet, a massage therapist, a groom, an auto repair guy and your personal hair stylist in your rolodex. Better they do those things than you in most cases.

<u>Because I am an equestrian myself.</u> I know as horsepeople we have our own language that we use – we use terms within our industry that mean something specific only to us. We know merely by how those terms are used if somebody is savvy or not to "our" horse language, and therefore, how much of an expert they are. I also know that within each discipline and sport we have terms that are even more specific. I am sensitive to that, I know what I don't know, and that *your* terminology needs to be reflected in your book.

<u>Because I offer a 7-Way, 100% Money-back, satisfaction guarantee</u> – Remember, you get what you pay for. I personally guarantee that you'll:

1. NOT have to write the book yourself.
2. Get your rough draft within 7-10 days of our final interview
3. Have final say over what is published.

4. Approve of the cover, and that I'll have several options for you within just a few days of our interview.
5. Have books in your hands, provided you get feedback to me in a timely manner, within 4-6 weeks of our initial interview.
6. Be so amazed at the results you see in your business stemming from publishing your book that you'll happily leave me a glowing endorsement.
7. ROI that makes you happy that you invested.

Try finding **any** ghostwriter or marketing specialist who offers ANY kind of guarantee – they are few and far between.

NOTES:_____

_____

_____

_____

_____

WHAT IS YOUR PROCESS?

Once I've given you the green light and accepted you as a client, we schedule an interview by phone.

1. I'll outline the milestones and when payments are due.
2. We'll go through your answers to the Transformation exercises in this book, (plus a few more), so I understand your business and your objectives completely.
3. Then we set up the structure of the book, and I ask questions as we go, which is the content.
4. We can spend up to 4 hours total interviewing – these may be 30-minute, 60-minute or up to 2-hour blocks of time.
5. I'll write a rough draft of the book, and send it to you for approval. You'll also get sample covers to approve.

6. I finish up the manuscript, get it printed, and send you a supply of books.

If you opt for a premium package, we determine exactly what you require, and then set up that marketing.

NOTES:_____

_____

_____

_____

_____

_____

_____

_____

_____

_____

_____

_____

_____

_____

Consultation Gift Certificate

Good For One Session Consultation

With Patricia Reszetylo

$197 VALUE/45 MINUTES

★ ★ ★ ★ ★

Strategy Session Where We'll

Explore Your Business, Work Out A Strategy That

Sets You Up As An Authority In Your Niche, And

Determines If We Can Work Together.

APPLY TODAY

http://PatriciaReszetylo.com/marketing-book

President

Next Step:

First, I suggest thinking about WHO the book is for. Are you writing this for:

- Prospective clients (consumers)?
- Prospective clinic organizers?
- Some other segment or group of customer?

The target market will determine our title and content. You wouldn't talk to a clinic participant about the same topics as you would somebody interested in organizing a clinic with you. So first we determine the audience.

Next we need a great title for your book. Here are a few suggestions to get you started – just tick the ones you think are interesting:

- ☐ What To Know About Choosing The Best (your specialty) Clinician in The (your area)
- ☐ (_____) That Other (_____) Don't Want You To Know About
- ☐ How To Confidently Host a Profitable Clinic With (clinician name)
- ☐ How To Confidently Choose The Best (discipline) Clinician For You And Your Horse
- ☐ How To Confidently Choose The Best (_____)
- ☐ How To (get this great benefit)
- ☐ Top (#) Of Ways To (get a benefit your training provides)
- ☐ (#) Things Your Current (clinician, trainer, instructor) Won't Tell You
- ☐ How To (do something) (fast, easy, cheap)
- ☐ How To (deal with a common problem)
- ☐ How Hosting A Clinic With (Name) Brings New Clients To Your Facility
- ☐ How (your solution) (provides an awesome benefit)
- ☐ How (your solution) (provides an awesome benefit) Without (common drawback)
- ☐ Using An Outside Clinician To Dramatically Boost Your Facility's Business
- ☐ Using (your solution) To (provide specific benefit)

- ☐ The Stable Manager's Guide To Hosting A Memorable Clinic That Participants Will Ask For Over And Over
- ☐ The (target audience)'s Guide To (what you do)

Think about the benefits your product or service provides, and the problems you solve for your clients. Then make it fast, easy, simple.

Remember, your book is to establish your authority, credibility, and expertise. It must properly educate your target audience with the things they need to know before they can make a decision, and it must motivate them to work with you. What questions do you WANT people to ask? What questions do your IDEAL clients ask?

It's also a device we can use to bring up and handle the objections people often bring up during the sales process. This will help you streamline closing sales, saving you time and making you money.

Then, to apply for your consultation session, please visit the website at http://PatriciaReszetylo.com/marketing-book, where you'll:

- Learn more about the process
- **Fill out and submit** the application.
- **Give me a few days** to go over your application and see if we fit.
- **If we ARE a fit,** we'll set up an appointment for your initial phone interview, and you'll get your homework assignment.

If we are NOT a fit, I'll let you know. I'll not waste your valuable time.

CONCLUSION

Navigating the marketing for your facility, services, product or sponsorship opportunity is tricky, even though the recession has passed. Your IDEAL clients ARE out there – but you have to PROVE your value to them.

You need a marketing strategy that:

- *Sets you apart from the herd,*
- *Positions* you as an authority in your niche,
- *Presents you as the only logical option* for your market, and
- *Doesn't interfere with your daily duties* or distract you from what you do best.

The properly written book, coupled with proper direct response marketing and website does that heavy lifting for you.

Are you ready to take your facility's marketing up a significant notch? Are you ready to make a REAL splash in the marketplace? Ready to stop competing with other facilities in your area, and REALLY establish yours as the ONE-AND-ONLY place to go for your sport/discipline?

If you're ready to move ahead, then take the NEXT STEP – connect with me and get started building your future.

I look forward to hearing from you, learning more about your business, and how I can best serve you!

Patricia Reszetylo,
Author of What To Know Before Marketing Your Clinician, Coaching, or Instruction Horse Business

Bonus Chapter #2:

Repurposing Content

What Is Repurposed Content?

Repurposed content is content that once created is used in a variety of ways. For example, you do an interview with somebody for your blog. You were perceptive, and recorded it. Now you could just post it on your blog, and be done with it, or you could:

- Get it transcribed, and
    - Written up as blog posts for the next several weeks.
    - Use it in a print or email newsletter.
    - Format the transcription nicely, and make a lead-generation ebook out of it.
    - Format it differently, and make an actual book (or a chapter in a book).
    - This book could be published on CreateSpace – and then placed on Amazon, also turned into a Kindle book.
    - Use bits on your various social media, such as Facebook, Twitter, Quora, Pinterest, Reddit, Tumblr, Flickr, and more.
- Turn it into a video, and put it on YouTube, Vimeo, Viddler, and more.
- As well as many more useful, engagement building, traffic driving, places.

Why Should I repurpose content?

There are many good reasons to repurpose content. One of the primary reason is so that you can do work one time – and then you can hand off that work to an assistant (or a team) and have IT work FOR you MANY times.

Another primary reason is that different people consume content in different ways – some people like to listen to podcasts, others prefer to read. Still others prefer video.

Other reasons for repurposing content is to reach people on different channels. Some people hang out on Facebook. Others are on Quora, and still others are on Twitter. Regardless of where they are, and how they like to consume content, you want to reach them.

And repurposing is how you do that.

How to Repurpose Content

Know Your Audience
First, it really helps to KNOW YOUR AUDIENCE. What format do they want their content in?

Give them that.

And then give it to them in a few more ways – you never know how you'll reach that next great client.

List of Ways and Places to Repurpose Content

a) **Newsletters** – Email, Print. Use transcribed pieces in your newsletters, whether they're online, email, or printed-and-mailed. You'll save a ton of time creating content for those, and as you already know your people like it, can give it to them in a format they're familiar with.

b) **Online Social media** – Pinterest, Facebook, Twitter, Google+, LinkedIn, BarnMice, YouTube, others. Where do you already have a presence? Have your social media person (or team) publish your content over a period of time. They'll appreciate the time they save having to come up with fresh content, your audience will appreciate the information. Depending on where it's published, it may take different forms, as we'll see in a moment.

c) **Publish Online** – Besides mainstream social media, there are tons of places to publish. Hand this list to your social media team – you'll need one to reach all these, and have them get cracking on it.

What will actually happen for most clinicians, is that you'll have a conference with your social media person, and together you'll determine objectives, and then choose a few to use.

http://coschedule.com/blog/repurpose-your-content/

~SOCIAL MEDIA~
1. Medium.com
2. SocialMediaToday.com
3. GrowthHackers.com
4. InBound.org
5. BizSugar.com
6. Reddit.com
7. News.ycombinator.com
8. Examiner.com
9. Business2Community.com
10. Quora.com
11. specialedition.linkedin.com/publishing/
12. Plus.google.com
13. StumbleUpon.com/pd/
14. LinkedIn Groups

~ ONLINE COURSES ~
15. Udemy.com
16. SkillShare.com
17. Guides.co
18. Helpouts By Google

~ CREATE SLIDEDECKS ~
19. SlideDeck.com
20. SlideWorld.com

21. SlideBloom.com
22. Scribd.com

~ INFOGRAPHICS ~

23. SlideShare.com
24. Visual.ly
25. Scribd.com
26. Pinterest.com
27. Tumblr.com
28. Google+
29. Flickr.com
30. DailyInfoGraphic.com
31. CoolInfoGraphics.com
32. InfographicsArchive.com
33. InfographicJournal.com
34. InfographicsShowcase.com

~ AUDIO/VISUAL VERSIONS ~

35. YouTube.com
36. Vimeo.com
37. Viddler.com
38. iTunes Podcast
39. Webinars – we've already touched on this.

~EBOOKS ~

40. **Regular ebooks** or whitepaper, depending on who you are targeting – use to build list, as bonus for course, etc.
41. **Kindle** books
42. **iBooks from Apple** – for iOS devices
43. **email course** – I've had good luck with this strategy before.

2. Tools to use – http://www.outbrain.com/blog/2014/07/23-tools-for-repurposing-content.html

APPENDIX

Sample Publicity and Photo Release Form

I hereby grant to the [business name] ([shortened business name]) the absolute and irrevocable right and unrestricted permission to use my name, likeness, image, voice, and/or appearance as such may be embodied in any photos, video recordings, audiotapes, digital images, and the like, taken or made on behalf of the [shortened business name] or its partners. I agree that the [shortened business name] has complete ownership of such material and can use said material for any purpose consistent with the [shortened business name]'s mission. These uses include, but are not limited to, videos, publications, advertisements, news releases, Web sites, and any promotional or educational materials in any medium. I acknowledge that I will not receive any compensation for the use of such images, video, likeness, etc. I hereby release and discharge the [shortened business name], and its agents, representatives and assignees from any and all claims and demands arising out of or in connection with the use of my name, likeness, image, voice and/or appearance, including any and all claims for invasion of privacy, right of publicity, misappropriation or misuse of image, and/or defamation. I represent that I am over the age of eighteen (18) years and that I have read the foregoing and fully understand its contents.* This release shall be binding upon me, my heirs, legal representatives, and assigns. This agreement is being made and entered into under the laws of the State of [business state] and shall be governed and interpreted in accordance with the laws of said state. This agreement embodies the entire agreement of the parties (subject and photographer). No modification of this agreement shall be of any effect unless itis made in writing and signed by all of the parties to the agreement. Name (Printed):

_____ Signature:

_____ Date: _____ * If the person signing is under the age of 18, consent from a parent or guardian is needed. I hereby certify that I am the parent or legal guardian of

_____, named above, and do hereby give my consent without reservation to the foregoing on behalf of this individual. Parent/Guardian's Name (Printed):

_____ Parent/Guardian's Signature: _____ Date:_____

NOTES:_____

_____

_____

_____

_____

_____

_____

_____

_____

_____

_____

_____

_____

---

[i] Did you figure it out? The pink, clapping bunny, aka, The Energizer Bunny, sells Energizer Batteries. I know, I usually forget it too!

www.ingramcontent.com/pod-product-compliance
Lightning Source LLC
Chambersburg PA
CBHW061442180526
45170CB00004B/1519